W9-AWR-857

Columbus Day

Dennis Brindell Fradin

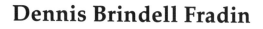

—Best Holiday Books—

Enslow Publishers, Inc.

44 Fadem Road	PO Box 38
Box 699	Aldershot
Springfield, NJ 07081	Hants GU12 6BP
USA	UK

> *For my wonderful mother-in-law,*
> *Elsie Ruth Bloom*

Library of Congress Cataloging-in-Publication Data
Fradin, Dennis B.
     Columbus Day / by Dennis B. Fradin.
         p. cm. — (Best holiday books)
     Includes index.
     Summary: Discusses how the achievements of the man credited with discovering
America led to the present-day celebration of his landing in the New World.
     ISBN 0-89490-233-4
     1. Columbus Day—Juvenile literature. 2. Columbus, Christopher—
Juvenile literature. 3. America—Discovery and exploration—
Spanish—Juvenile literature. [1. Columbus Day. 2. Columbus,
Christopher. 3. America—Discovery and exploration—Spanish.]
I. Title. II. Series: Fradin, Dennis B. Best holiday books.
E120.F8 1990
970.01'5—dc20   89-7663
                                           CIP
                                           AC

Printed in the United States of America

10 9 8 7 6

Illustration Credits:
Bahamas Ministry of Tourism Central Photographic Services: p. 29; The British
Library: p. 20; Columbus Day Parade sponsored by Joint Civic Committee of Italian
Americans: p. 44; Tom Dunnington: pp. 10-11, 26, 35; Giraudon/Art Resource, NY:
p. 13; Historical Pictures Service, Chicago: p. 16; By courtesy of the Italian Govern-
ment Travel Office (E.N.I.T.): pp. 8, 41; Library of Congress: pp. 18, 22, 24, 28, 32;
The Metropolitan Museum of Art, Gift of J. Pierpont Morgan, 1900: p. 4; National
Portrait Gallery, Smithsonian Institution, Washington, D.C.: p. 43; Scala/Art
Resource, NY: p. 12; Servizio Beni Culturali del Comune di Genova: p. 36.

Cover Illustration by Charlott Nathan

Contents

This portrait of Christopher Columbus was painted by the Italian artist Sebastiano del Piombo in 1519. That was 13 years after Columbus died. No portrait of Columbus was done during his lifetime.

Honoring Christopher Columbus

Christopher Columbus was a great explorer. In 1492 he sailed from Europe to the Americas. Columbus was not the first European in the Americas. But he was the first to start permanent settlement of the New World.

Columbus is honored in many ways for his deeds. The South American nation of Colombia was named for him. Columbus, Ohio, and Columbus, Georgia, are two of the U.S. cities named for him. The United States also has a national holiday to honor Christopher Columbus.

Called Columbus Day, this holiday is held on the second Monday in October. That time of year was picked because Columbus first landed in the New World in mid-October of 1492. The days before Columbus Day are a good time to learn about why we honor this great explorer.

Christopher Columbus's Dream

Christopher Columbus was born in 1451 in Genoa, Italy. As a child, he helped his father, who was a wool weaver. Christopher did not want to become a weaver, though. Instead, he hoped to go to sea.

Sometime between the ages of 10 and 14, Christopher made his first voyage. It was probably a short one from Genoa to a nearby port. He probably worked for his father a few more years while making other voyages from time to time.

Christopher began making longer voyages when he was about 20. On one trip he sailed to France and Tunisia. On another he went to an

It is thought that Christopher Columbus was born in this house in Genoa, Italy.

island between Greece and Turkey. He learned a great deal about ships and sailing on these trips.

Many details about Columbus's life are not known. For example, we know that by late 1476 he lived in Portugal. But we are not sure how he got there. Some historians say that in the summer of 1476 Columbus was on a ship bound for England. Off the coast of Portugal, the ship was attacked and sunk. Although wounded, Christopher grabbed a piece of wood and paddled to shore.

By the spring of 1477, Christopher Columbus was in Lisbon, the capital of Portugal and a great seafaring city. Bartholomew Columbus, who was one of Christopher's two younger brothers, already lived in Lisbon. Bartholomew worked in a chart (map) shop. Ship captains who needed to know the best sailing routes bought these charts. The brothers may have opened their own chart shop in Lisbon. And Christopher sometimes sailed on ships going out of Lisbon.

While living in Lisbon, Christopher had an idea that changed his life. Portugal wanted to obtain gold, spices, and other goods from Asian lands. It was hard to reach Asia over land, so the Portuguese hoped to find a way to sail there. Most explorers tried to reach Asia by sailing south and then east around Africa. This was

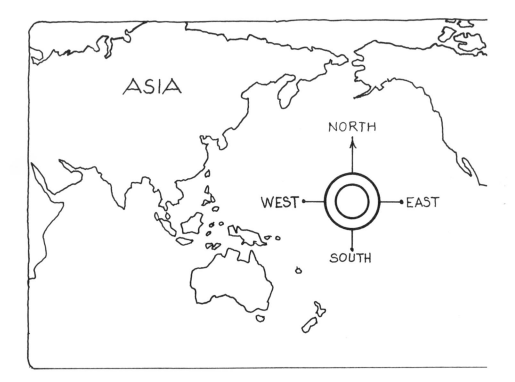

COLUMBUS'S PLANNED ROUTE TO ASIA (DOTTED LINE)

finally done in the late 1400s. Sailing around Africa was long and dangerous, though. Columbus thought there was an easier route to Asia.

People had known that the earth is round since ancient times. Because the earth is round, any place on it can be reached from the east or the west. Columbus figured that sailing west

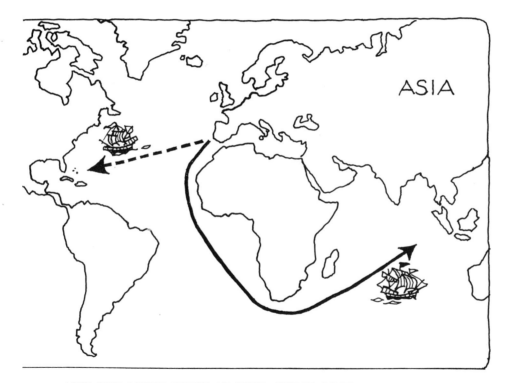

AND THE MORE POPULAR IDEA (SOLID LINE)
Columbus didn't know that the Americas were in the way.

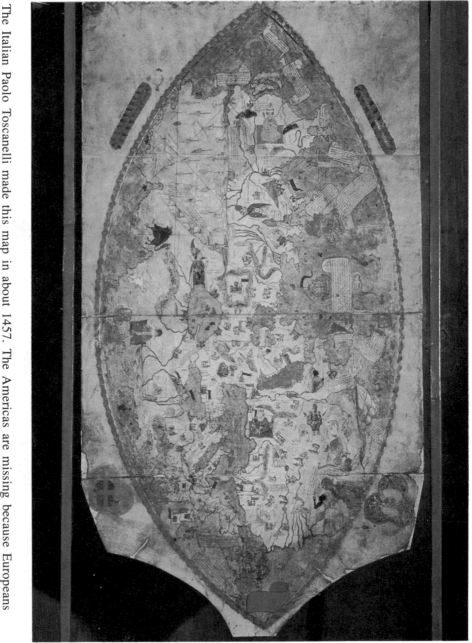

The Italian Paolo Toscanelli made this map in about 1457. The Americas are missing because Europeans did not know about them then.

Lisbon as it looked around Columbus's time

to Asia would be easier than sailing around Africa.

Christopher Columbus studied maps and geography books. He became more and more convinced that he could reach Asia by sailing west. He did not know it, but he had made two big mistakes. He thought Asia was just 3,000 miles west of Lisbon. It was over three times that far. Second, a big landmass blocked the way to Asia. It was made up of North and South America.

Long before, in about 1000 A.D., the Viking Leif Ericson had sailed to North America. The Vikings were from Norway and nearby lands. Ericson probably landed in Canada. Today, we consider him the first known European explorer of the Americas. But Leif Ericson never realized where he had gone. And by Columbus's time, knowledge of Ericson's trip to North America was lost.

Selling the Dream

In about 1479, Christopher Columbus married Felipa Perestrello e Moniz. They moved to Felipa's home in Portugal's Madeira Islands, off the northwest coast of Africa.

While living in the Madeiras, Christopher continued to go to sea. Once he led a voyage to Africa's west coast. But he did not forget his dream of a westward voyage to Asia. The problem was, the expedition would be very costly. He needed several ships to attempt the voyage. That way if one ship sank, the sailors could be rescued.

Christopher Columbus began asking European rulers to pay for his voyage. In 1484, he asked Portugal's King John II. The next year was awful for Columbus. His wife, Felipa, died either in 1485 or shortly before. And in 1485 King John II refused to give him money.

Columbus then decided to seek help in Spain. He and his five-year-old son, Diego, sailed to Palos, Spain. They walked four miles to the La Rábida monastery, which took in boarders. The Catholic priests and brothers at La Rábida took Diego in as a student. Columbus then began

Christopher and Diego Columbus at La Rábida

seeking help from Spain's Queen Isabella and King Ferdinand.

It took Columbus a year just to meet Isabella. The queen liked the red-haired Italian. But her aides said she should not pay for Columbus's voyage. The world was much bigger than Columbus thought, they said. (They were right!) Asia was much farther away than Columbus thought. (They were right again!) How could ships go that far? How could they carry enough food for the sailors? Portugal's King John II had refused him for the same reasons.

Isabella did not give him a definite "No." She even gave him money to live on while she thought more about his plan. While Isabella thought about it, Columbus tried Portugal's king again. Bartholomew sought help in England and France. Neither brother had any luck.

Christopher kept pestering Isabella. Finally, she said she might help him once Spain won a war it was fighting. By early 1492, the fighting was over. Feeling hopeful, Columbus visited Isabella and Ferdinand. The queen favored Columbus's plan. Some advisers were opposed, though, and Ferdinand showed little interest. This time the "No" looked final.

Christopher had been promoting his idea for almost 10 years, with no success. Many people would have given up by this time, but not Chris-

Columbus speaking to Queen Isabella and her court

topher Columbus. He planned to go to France and offer his idea to the French king again.

Meanwhile, a royal official came to Isabella just after Columbus left her. He was treasurer Luis de Santangel, and he believed in Columbus's idea. Santangel advised Isabella to help Christopher Columbus. Isabella did not need much convincing. The queen sent a messenger, who found Columbus at a nearby village. After years of disappointment, Christopher Columbus was going on his dream voyage!

Old Spanish gold coin showing heads of Ferdinand and Isabella

The Famous Voyage to America

The expedition was to sail from Palos in south-western Spain. Columbus was provided with three ships—the *Niña*, the *Pinta*, and the *Santa María*. The seafaring Pinzón family helped him gather sailors. Including Columbus, 90 men would sail the three ships.

Compared to modern ocean liners, Columbus's ships were tiny. The largest, the *Santa María*, was only about 80 feet long. Forty men, including Columbus, sailed on the *Santa María*, which was the slowest of the three ships. The *Pinta* was only about 70 feet long. It was the fastest of the ships and carried 26 men. Columbus considered the *Niña* the best of his three ships. It was about the size of the *Pinta* and carried 24 men.

The three ships left Palos on August 3, 1492. About a week later they reached the Canary Islands, off Africa's northwest coast. Water and food were obtained in the Canaries, and the *Pinta* was repaired. On September 6, the expedition left the Canaries. The men would not see land again for over a month.

Columbus setting off on his famous voyage. He is holding Queen Isabella's hand.

Motors for ships did not yet exist. Columbus's ships moved when the wind pushed at their sails. For most of the trip, there was a good wind from the east. The ships averaged about 100 miles a day.

Christopher Columbus was thrilled to be making his voyage. But as time passed, many of his men became scared. They thought they might starve before reaching Asia. They wondered if they could return home even if they reached Asia. And some of them probably believed the old stories about sea monsters in far-off waters.

By early October, some of the men were begging Columbus to turn around. He refused. The men needed Columbus to find the way home. Otherwise they might have killed him and turned the ships around themselves.

By October 9, Columbus knew that his men were about to revolt. On that day or the next, Columbus made a promise. Unless they reached land in three days, they would return home.

Columbus's three ships—*Santa María* (center), *Niña* (left), and *Pinta* (right)

On October 11, they saw branches floating past the ships. They also saw a stick that looked as though a human being had carved it. The men went to sleep feeling hopeful that they were near land. At about 10 that night, Columbus thought he saw a light far to the west. The great moment came four hours later.

The date was October 12, 1492. The time was two o'clock in the morning. In the moonlight, the *Pinta*'s lookout saw land rising out of the sea. *"Tierra! Tierra!"* he called, meaning "Land! Land!" They had reached an island southeast of the Florida coast.

The island was one of the Bahamas, but which one is not known. Some say it was Samana Cay. Others claim it was Watling Island. In any case, Columbus and his men had reached the New World. Columbus had arrived on October 12. That is why Columbus Day is now held in early or mid-October in the United States.

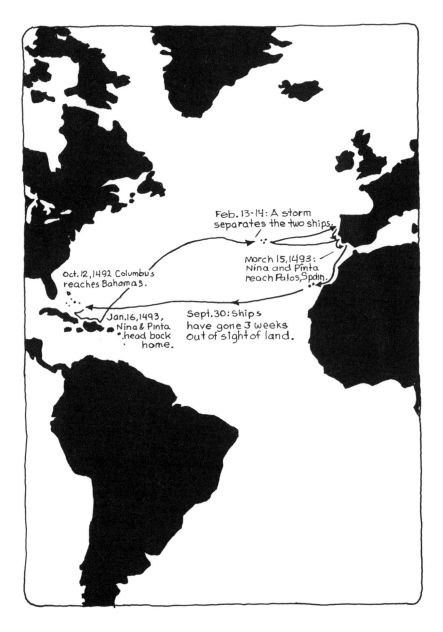

Feb. 13-14: A storm separates the two ships.

March 15, 1493: Nina and Pinta reach Palos, Spain.

Oct. 12, 1492 Columbus reaches Bahamas.

Jan. 16, 1493, Nina & Pinta head back home.

Sept. 30: Ships have gone 3 weeks out of sight of land.

ROUTE OF COLUMBUS'S FAMOUS VOYAGE

Indians and Discoveries

The men stayed on the ships that night. In the morning, some islanders came out onto the beach. They looked friendly and even brought gifts for the newcomers. Columbus and some others went ashore to meet them.

The Asian lands around China and Japan were called the Indies then. Thinking he was in the Indies, Columbus called the people Indians. These Indians were peaceful farmers. They gave Columbus and his men food and water. The Indians also showed the visitors around the island.

Columbus liked the Indians. But when he saw that their jewelry was made of gold, he

Columbus's arrival on New World soil

Tourists inspect the spot where Columbus may have arrived in the Bahamas.

began making evil plans. He decided that the Indians should be the slaves of the Europeans who would settle in this region. The Indians would mine gold for the Europeans and do their other work. Columbus also hoped the Indians would become Christians. He felt they would gain more from Christianity than they would lose by becoming slaves.

Before leaving the island, Columbus kidnapped a few Indians. He wanted them to guide him to other islands. And he wanted to show them off back in Spain.

Still thinking he was in Asia, Columbus visited more islands in a search for China. He explored Cuba and the island of Hispaniola. He and his men found some gold and met many friendly Indians.

On Christmas Eve, disaster struck. Off what is now Haiti on the island of Hispaniola, the *Santa María* was wrecked. The *Pinta* was off exploring, and the *Niña* could not carry all the *Santa María*'s men. Columbus had to leave 40 men behind on the island. They were to build a settlement and find gold. Columbus then headed home.

The trip back across the Atlantic Ocean was very hard. The ships ran into storms. The *Niña,* with Columbus aboard, nearly sank. The two ships finally reached Palos, Spain, on March 15, 1493.

Columbus walked a long way to Ferdinand and Isabella's court with his Indians and some sailors. People gathered to cheer him and see the Indians. The king and queen gave Columbus many honors and told him to make a second voyage. They wanted him to build Spanish colonies in the New World.

Columbus showing his Indian captives to Ferdinand and Isabella

Columbus's Three Other Voyages to America

Columbus made three more voyages to America. On his second voyage (1493–1496) he discovered Puerto Rico and Jamaica. On the third voyage (1498–1500) he discovered Venezuela in South America. On the fourth (1502–1504) he explored parts of Central America. Columbus came to realize that he had found what he called an "Other World." But he was not sure where it was.

Thousands of Spaniards moved to the New World during and soon after Columbus's last three voyages. This began Spanish colonization of the Americas. Spain took over much of Central and South America and many islands off the coast. Tragically, the Spaniards enslaved and killed thousands of Indians while doing this.

On Columbus's last trip, he and his men were stranded on Jamaica. Their food ran low. Columbus then did his famous "eclipse trick."

Columbus knew that the moon would be eclipsed on February 29, 1504. When that happens, the moon turns reddish because the earth's shadow passes over it. Columbus told the Indians on Jamaica that God would make the moon red because they would not give his men food. The moon changed color when Columbus said it would. The frightened Indians then gave Columbus the food his men needed.

After a year on Jamaica, Columbus and his men were rescued. They reached Spain in late 1504.

Columbus's famous "eclipse trick"

Portrait of Christopher Columbus in his last years

The Story of
Columbus Day

Christopher Columbus had been weakened by his many hardships. In the spring of 1506, he died in Spain at just 54 years of age. To the end, he was not sure where his "Other World" was located.

People soon realized that Columbus had found new continents. Some thought they should be named Columbia, after him. But the new lands were called the Americas. They were named for Amerigo Vespucci, who explored the New World soon after Columbus's first voyage.

After the United States was formed in 1776, people took interest in the nation's roots. On October 12, 1792, some people in New York

City honored the 300th anniversary of Columbus's famous landing in the Americas. This was the start of Columbus Day. But no yearly Columbus Day celebrations were held yet.

In 1892, people across the United States celebrated the 400th anniversary of Columbus's landing. Yearly Columbus Day celebrations were begun 28 later, in 1920. But Columbus Day was still not a legal national holiday. Various states held their own Columbus Day celebrations on October 12 of each year.

The U.S. Congress finally made Columbus Day a legal national holiday starting in 1971. The Congress also decided that Columbus Day would be held on the second Monday in October. That way people would have a three-day Columbus Day weekend.

Schoolchildren and Columbus Day

In early October, many children do Columbus Day projects in school. Their teachers read them stories about Christopher Columbus. The children then write their own stories about him. Some schoolchildren make drawings or even models of Columbus's ships—the *Niña,* the *Pinta,* and the *Santa María.* And some schools put on plays about Christopher Columbus and his famous 1492 voyage.

There are also several old rhymes about Christopher Columbus that children may learn for the holiday. Some, like the two below, are old playground rhymes that children may know better than their teachers:

In fourteen hundred ninety-two
Columbus sailed the ocean blue.

Columbus went to sea, sea, sea
To see what he could see, see, see,
But all that he could see, see, see,
Was the bottom of the deep blue sea, sea, sea.

Because Columbus was born in Italy, millions of Italian-Americans are especially proud of him. Some schools have an Italian Heritage week or month around the time of Columbus Day. Besides learning about Christopher Columbus, the children learn about other famous people of Italian background.

Columbus often sailed in the Mediterranean Sea.

The Second Monday in October

Columbus Day is a federal (national) holiday in the United States. There is no mail. U.S. government offices are closed. Most schools are closed, as are many businesses.

Many cities and towns hold Columbus Day parades. Some of them are led by men dressed up as Christopher Columbus. There may also be floats honoring Queen Isabella, who sent Columbus on his way, and the Indians who helped him in the New World.

One very interesting Columbus Day parade is held in Columbus, Ohio. Each year, people from all the U.S. cities and towns named Columbus are invited to take part in this parade.

In 1988, people from 13 cities and towns from around the country participated.

The year 1992 marks the 500th anniversary of Columbus's landing in America. Columbus probably never dreamed that people would be celebrating his achievement 500 years later. It will probably be celebrated for ages to come. For Columbus Day is a special time to honor the brave man who dreamed of a shortcut to Asia but found a New World.

Pen-and-ink portrait of Christopher Columbus

Chicago, Illinois, holds a yearly Columbus Day parade. The young people are dressed up as Christopher Columbus and Queen Isabella.

Glossary

anniversary—the day of the year on which a past event occurred

capital—the place where laws are made for a nation or state

continent—one of the earth's biggest landmasses

discover—to learn about something before anyone else does

eclipse—the blocking out of one heavenly body by another

expedition—a journey

explorer—someone who visits and studies unknown lands

Indies—an old name for the Asian lands around China and Japan

kidnap—to seize a person against his or her will

monastery—a place where men who have taken religious vows live apart from the world

New World—a nickname for the Americas

permanent—lasting

slaves—people who are owned by other people

thousand—ten hundred (1,000)

treasurer—a person who is in charge of money

voyage—this usually means a trip across the sea by ship

Index

Twin Branch School